Susanne Dorendorff
Dorendorff's Alphabet of Latin Cursive Script
in 30 Figures

Philipp

Susanne Dorendorff

Dorendorff's Alphabet of Latin Cursive Script

in 30 Figures

with 1.770 connetions

for the acquisition of handwriting skills in (almost) all
world languages

Bibliographic information of the German National Library.
The German National Library lists this publication in the German National Bibliography;
detailed bibliographic information can be found at http://dnb.de

ISBN 9783752846676

Contents

Latin Cursive Script

Handwriting is booming – 59 letters for (almost) all world languages

Individual handwriting guarantees privacy – the computer does the opposite.

The international writing technique of *connected* upper and lowercase letters (colloquially: Latin cursive script; in Germany: Latin Basic Script [LA]) has been successful for the past 500 years and is hence viewed by many generations in and almost all world languages as a reliable tool for thinking and communication. As a consequence of digitalisation, this way of writing is experiencing increasing success.

Both the alphabetisation of children through Latin cursive script and the importance of computers make this unique technique of international communication indispensable. Handwritten Latin cursive script is quick, individual and in most cases comes with privacy protection.

It has long become clear: Those who have mastered a quick handwriting are part of a network of communications that, unnoticed and confidentially, is forming worldwide connections. Digitalisation and globalisation indicate that the technique of handwriting is an absolute MUST for any modern-day individual.

Neither music nor singing, dancing, sculpture or drawing demand from their authors a similar degree of spontaneously authentic output as is the case with handwriting, which *emerges almost autonomously as from a bubbling spring.*
A lot is left to discover in this context.

The letters pictured in this booklet can be complemented manually with national or individual special characters. For this purpose, please use the added pages at the end of the alphabet.

And now: much success!

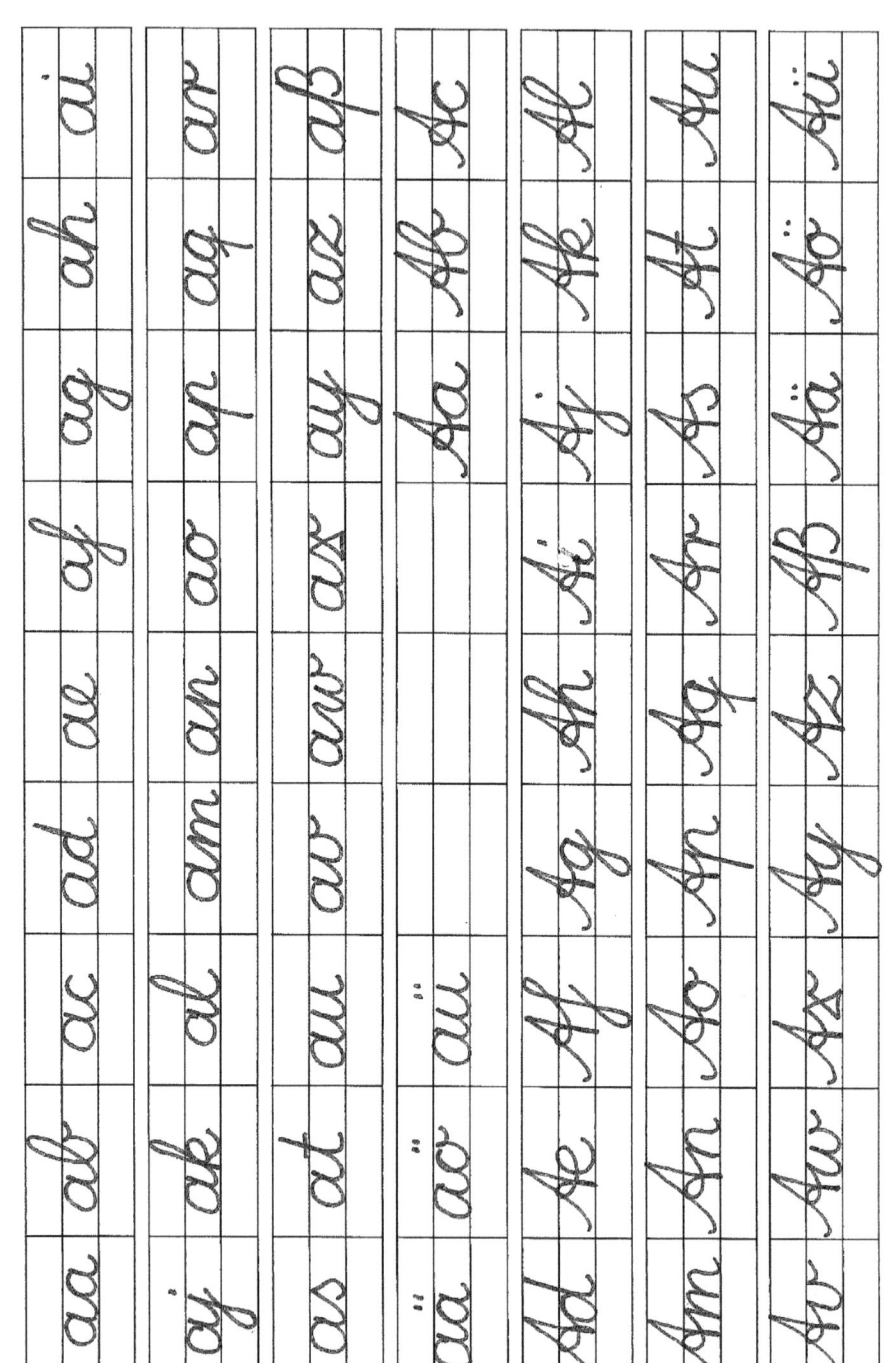

ba bä bc bd be bf bg bh bi

bj bk bl bm bn bo bp bq br

bs bt bu bv bw bx by bz bß

bä bö bü ba

Bd Be Bf Bg Bh Bi Bj Bk Bc

Bm Bn Bo Bp Bq Br Bs Bt Bu

Bv Bw Bx By Bz Bß Ba Bö Bü

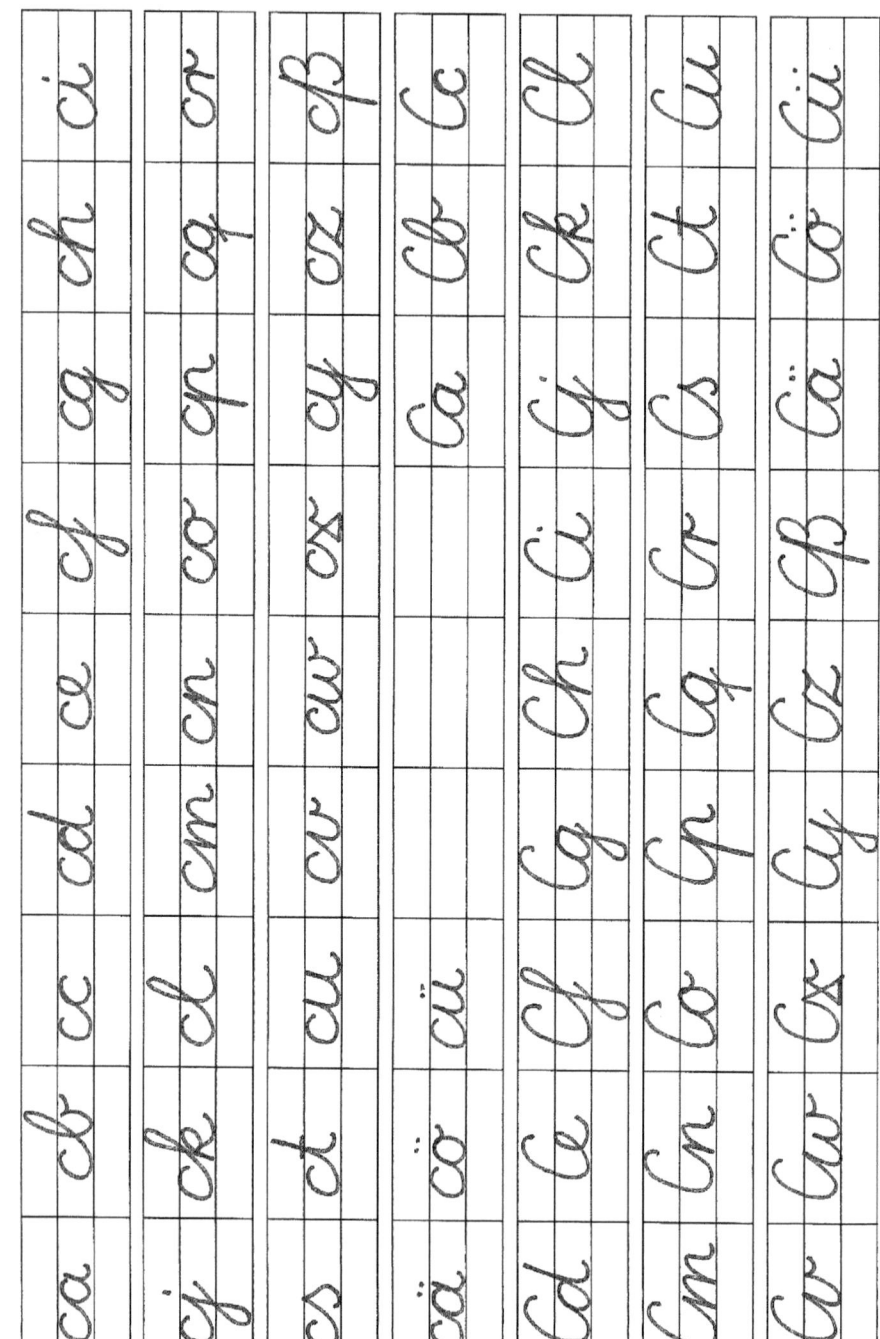

da db dc dd de df dg dh di

dj dk dl dm dn do dp dq dr

ds dt du dv dw dx dy dz dß

dä dö dü Da Db Dc

Dd De Df Dg Dh Di Dj Dk Dl

Dm Dn Do Dp Dq Dr Ds Dt Du

Dv Dw Dx Dy Dz Dß Dä Dö Dü

fa	fb	fc	fd	fe	ff	fg	fh	fi
fj	fk	fl	fm	fn	fo	fp	fq	fr
fs	ft	fu	fv	fw	fx	fy	fz	fß
fä	fö	fü				Fa	Fb	Fc
Fd	Fe	Ff	Fg	Fh	Fi	Fj	Fk	Fl
Fm	Fn	Fo	Fp	Fq	Fr	Fs	Ft	Fu
Fv	Fw	Fx	Fy	Fz	Fß	Fä	Fö	Fü

ga · gb · gc · gd · ge · gf · gg · gh · gi

gj · gk · gl · gm · gn · go · gp · gq · gr

gs · gt · gu · gv · gw · gx · gy · gz · gß

ga · go · gu · gs · gl · gz · gg · gß

Gd · Ge · Gf · Gg · Gh · Gi · Gk · Gb · Gc

Gm · Gn · Go · Gp · Gq · Gr · Gs · Gk · Ge

Gv · Gw · Gx · Gy · Gz · Gr · Gq · Gt · Gu

Gv · Gw · Gß · Gz · Gä · Gö · Gü

ha hb hc hd he hf hg hh hi

hi hj hk hl hm hn ho hp hq hr

hs ht hu hv hw hx hy hz hß

hä hö hü ha

Ha Hb Hc Hd He Hf Hg Hh Hi

Ha Hb Hc Hd He Hf Hg Hh Hi

Ha Hb Hc Hd He Hf Hg Hh Hi

Hä Hö Hü Ha Ho Hi

ka kb kc kd ke kf kg kh ki

kj kk kl km kn ko kp kq kr

ks kt ku kv kw kx ky kz kß

kä kö kü

Ka Kb Kc

Kd Ke Kf Kg Kh Ki Kj Kk Kl

Km Kn Ko Kp Kq Kr Ks Kt Ku

Kr Kw Kx Ky Kz Kß Kä Kö Kü

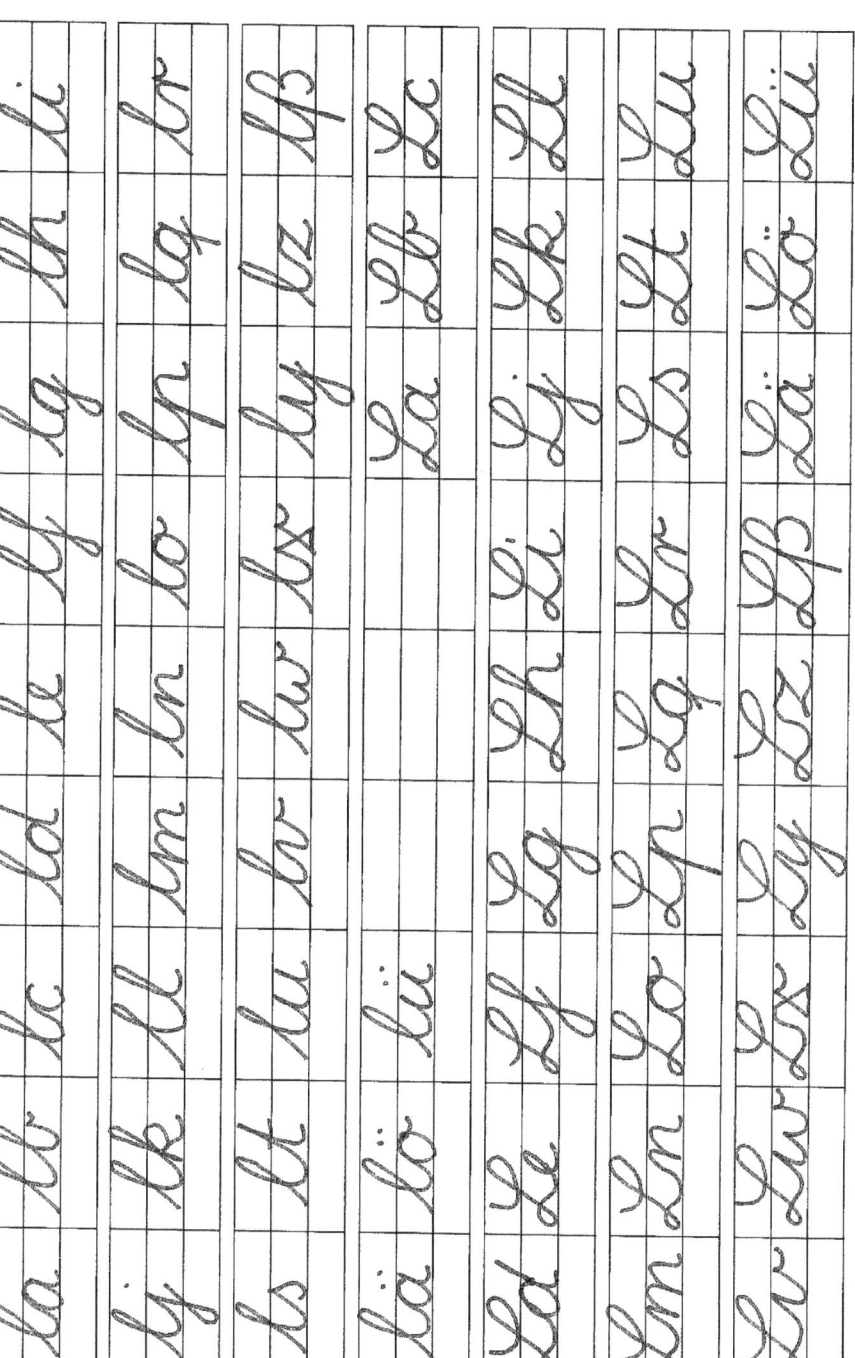

ma mb mc md me mf mg mh mi

mj mk ml mm mn mo mp mq mr

ms mt mu mm mn mo mp mq mf

mä mä mü mü

Md Me Mf Mg Mh Mi Mj Mc

M Mn Mo Mp Mq Mr Ms Mt Mu

Mr Mw Mx My Mz Mp Mö Mo Mü

na nb nc nd ne nf ng nh ni

nj nk nl nm nn no np nq nr

ns nt nu nv nw nx ny nz nß

nä nö nü

Nd Ne Nf Ng Nh Ni Nj Nk Nl Nc

Nm Nn No Np Nq Nr Ns Nt Nu

Nr Nw Nx Ny Nz Nä Nö Nü

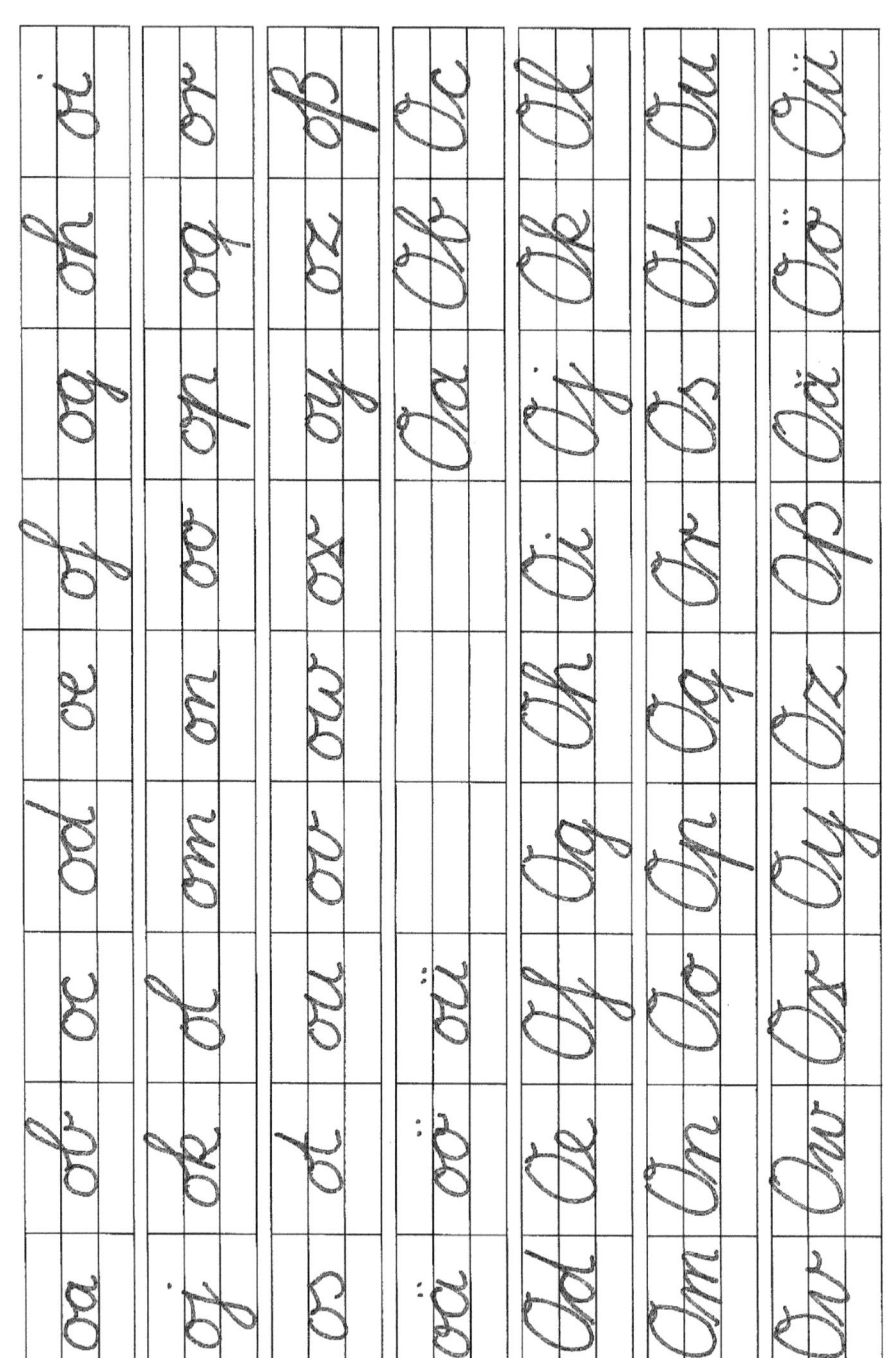

qua quä qué quä qui quä qui

quï quä qum quä quä quä quo

qus qut quä quo quä quä quß

quä quo quü Qua Qub Que

Que Auf Auh Aui Auj Auk Aul

Qum Quo Qup Aug Qug Qut Qua

Quo Qus Auy Auz Aus Out Qua

Quo Aus Auy Auz Auß Qua Quo

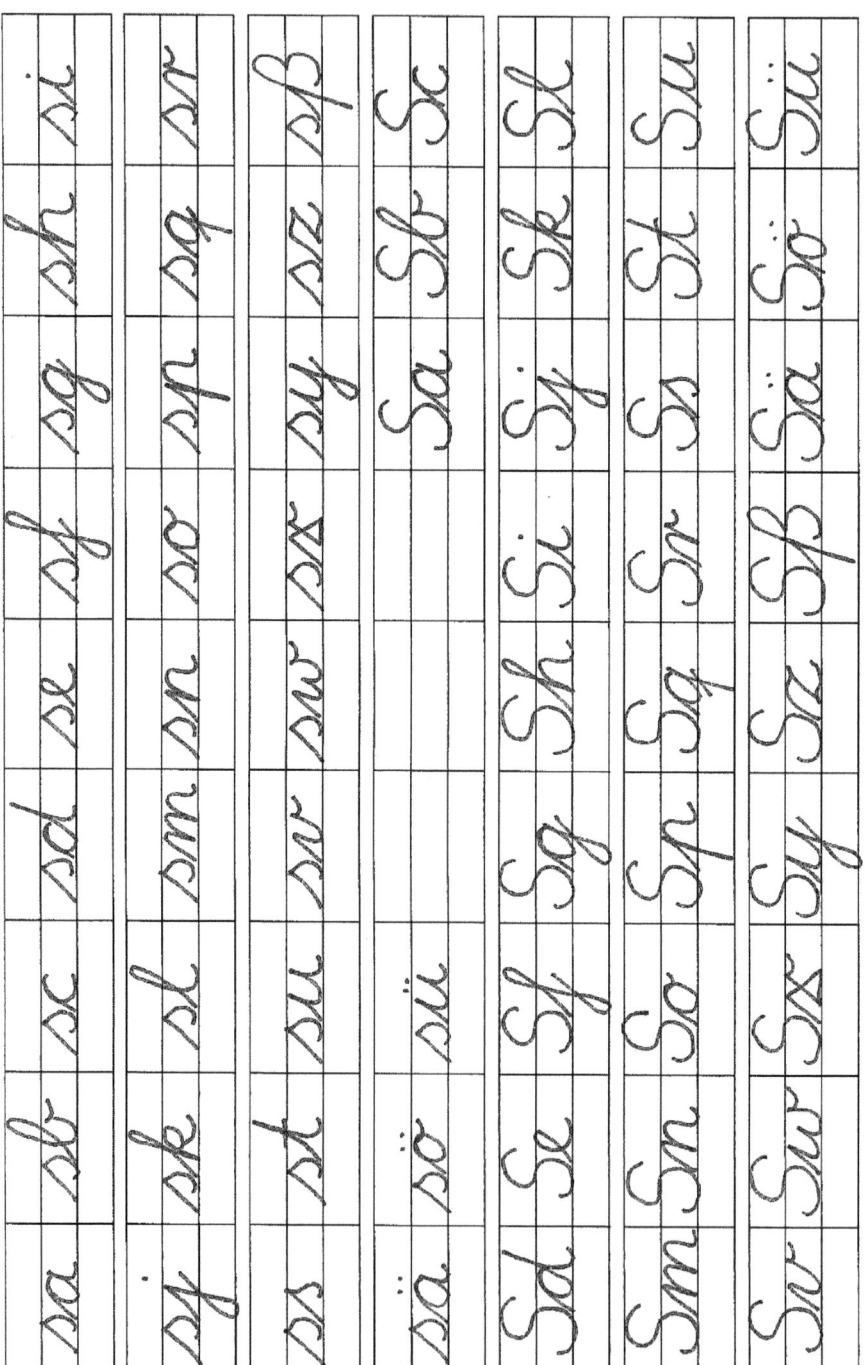

ta tb tc td te tf tg th ti
ty tk tl tm tn to tp tq tr
ts tt tu tv tw tx ty tz tß

tä tö tü

Td Te Tf Tg Th Ti Tk Tl
Tm Tn To Tp Tq Tr Ts Tt Tu
Tr Tw Tx Ty Tz Tä Tö Tü

ua	ub	uc	ud	ue	uf	ug	uh	ui
uj	uk	ul	um	un	uo	up	uq	ur
us	ut	uu	uv	uw	ux	uy	uz	uß
uä	uö	üü				Ua	Ub	Uc
Ud	Ue	Uf	Ug	Uh	Ui	Uj	Uk	Ul
Um	Un	Uo	Up	Uq	Ur	Us	Ut	Uu
Uv	Uw	Ux	Uy	Uz	Uß	Uä	Uö	Uü

va	vb	vc	vd	ve	vf	vg	vh	vi
vj	vk	vl	vm	vn	vo	vp	vq	vr
vs	vt	vu	vv	vw	vx	vy	vz	vß
vä	vö	vü				Va	Vb	Vc
Vd	Ve	Vf	Vg	Vh	Vi	Vj	Vk	Vl
Vm	Vn	Vo	Vp	Vq	Vr	Vs	Vt	Vu
Vv	Vw	Vx	Vy	Vz	Vß	Vä	Vö	Vü

xa	xb	xc	xd	xe	xf	xg	xh	xi
xj	xk	xl	xm	xn	xo	xp	xq	xr
xs	xt	xu	xv	xw	xx	xy	xz	xß
xä	xö	xü				Xa	Xb	Xc
Xd	Xe	Xf	Xg	Xh	Xi	Xj	Xk	Xl
Xm	Xn	Xo	Xp	Xq	Xr	Xs	Xt	Xu
Xv	Xw	Xx	Xy	Xz	Xß	Xä	Xö	Xü

Ця Цй Цс Цд Це Цф Цв Ци
Ця Цй Цк Цл Цм Цн Цо Цп
Цъ Цы Ць Цэ Цю Ця Ця Цб
Ця Ця Цш Цы Цо Цн Цз Цж
Цч Це Цф Цх Цц Цш Цщ Цъ
Цы Цм Цн Цо Цп Цр Ца Цб
Цъ Цы Цх Цы Цз Цж Цо Ци

za zb zc zd ze zf zg zh zi

zf zk zl zm zn zo zp zq zr

zs zt zu zv zw zx zy zß

za zo zu za zb zc

zd ze zf zg zh zi zk zl

zm zn zo zp zq zr zs zt zu

zu zv zw zx zy zß zz zö zü

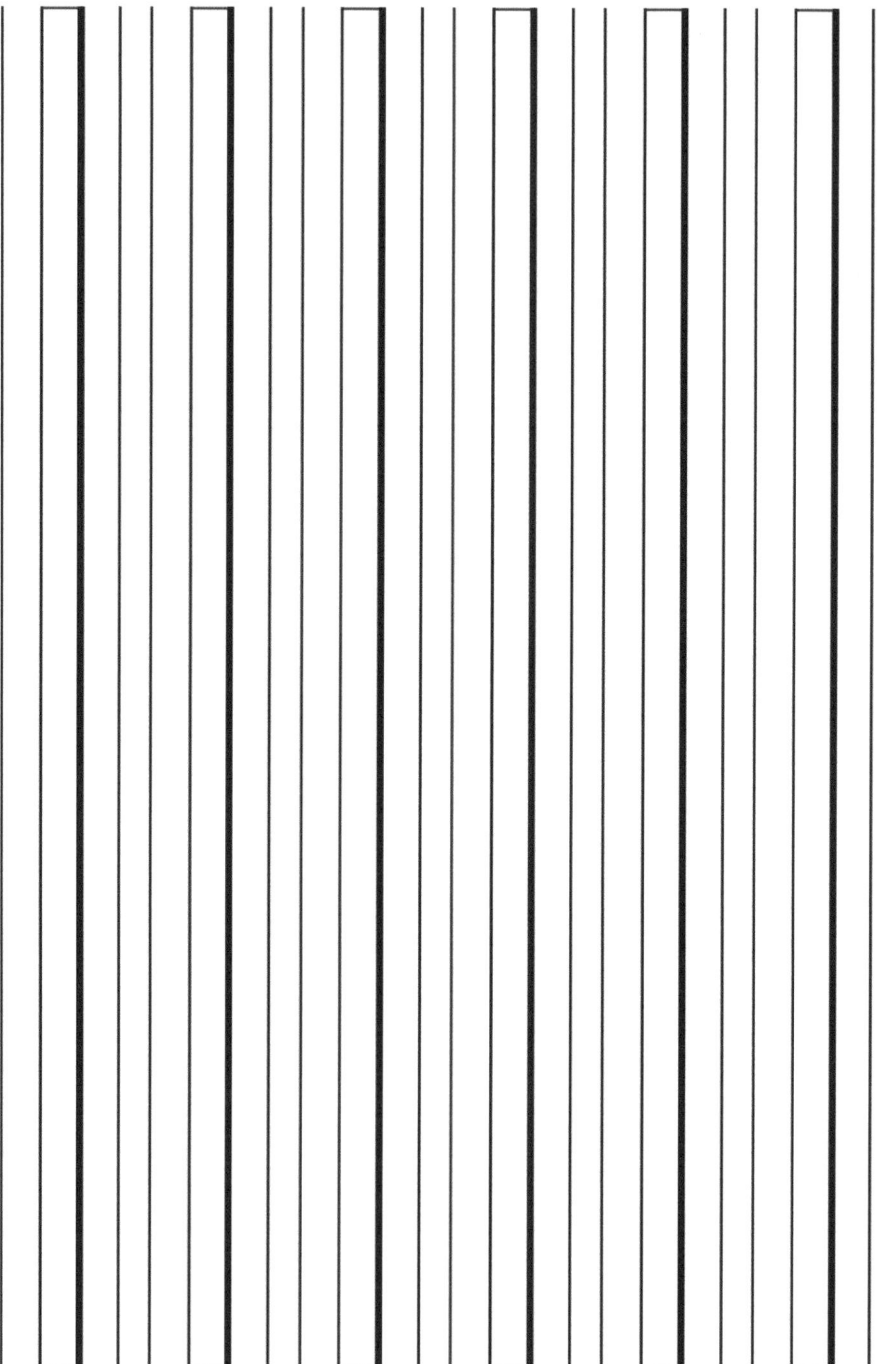

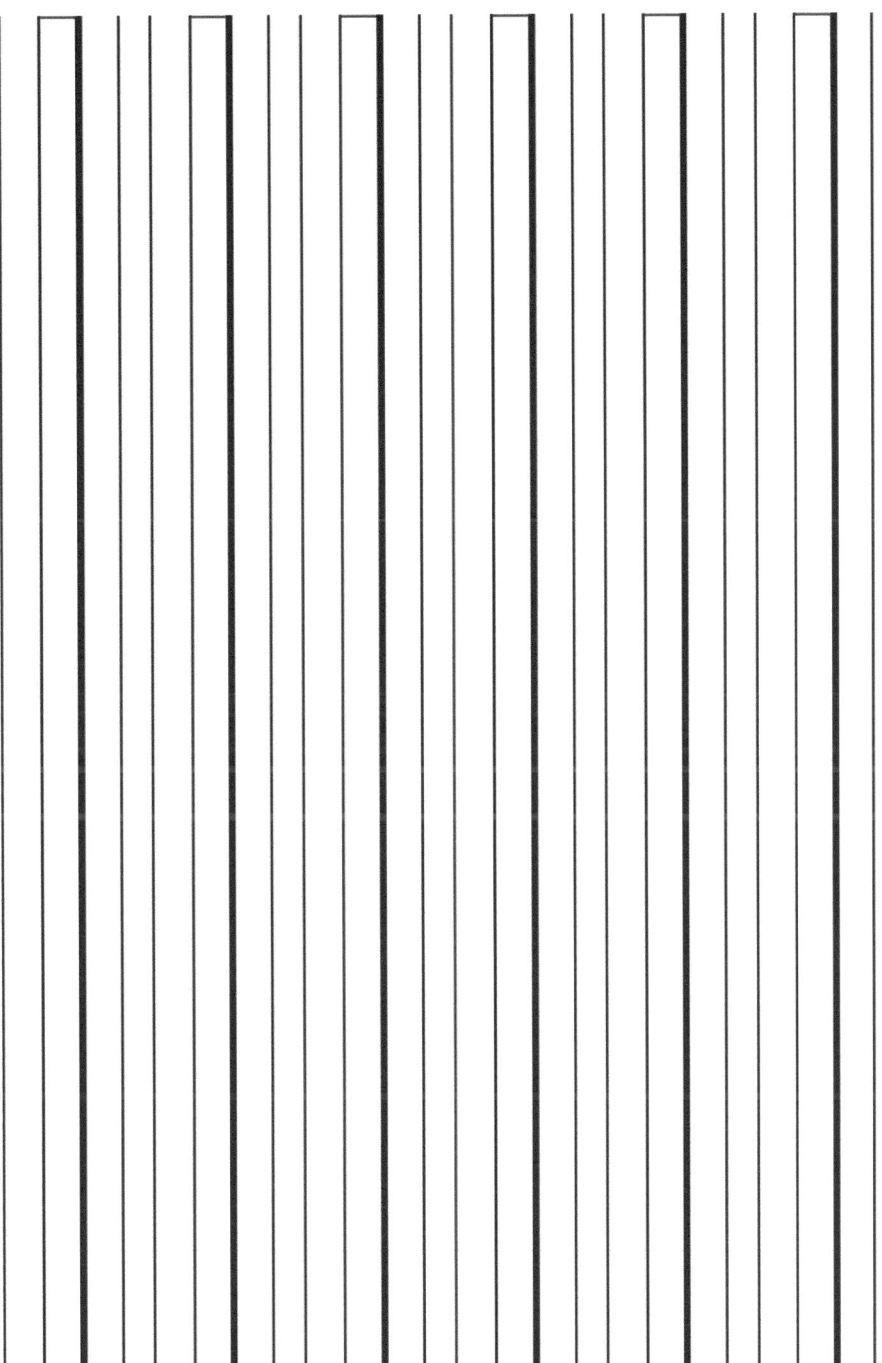

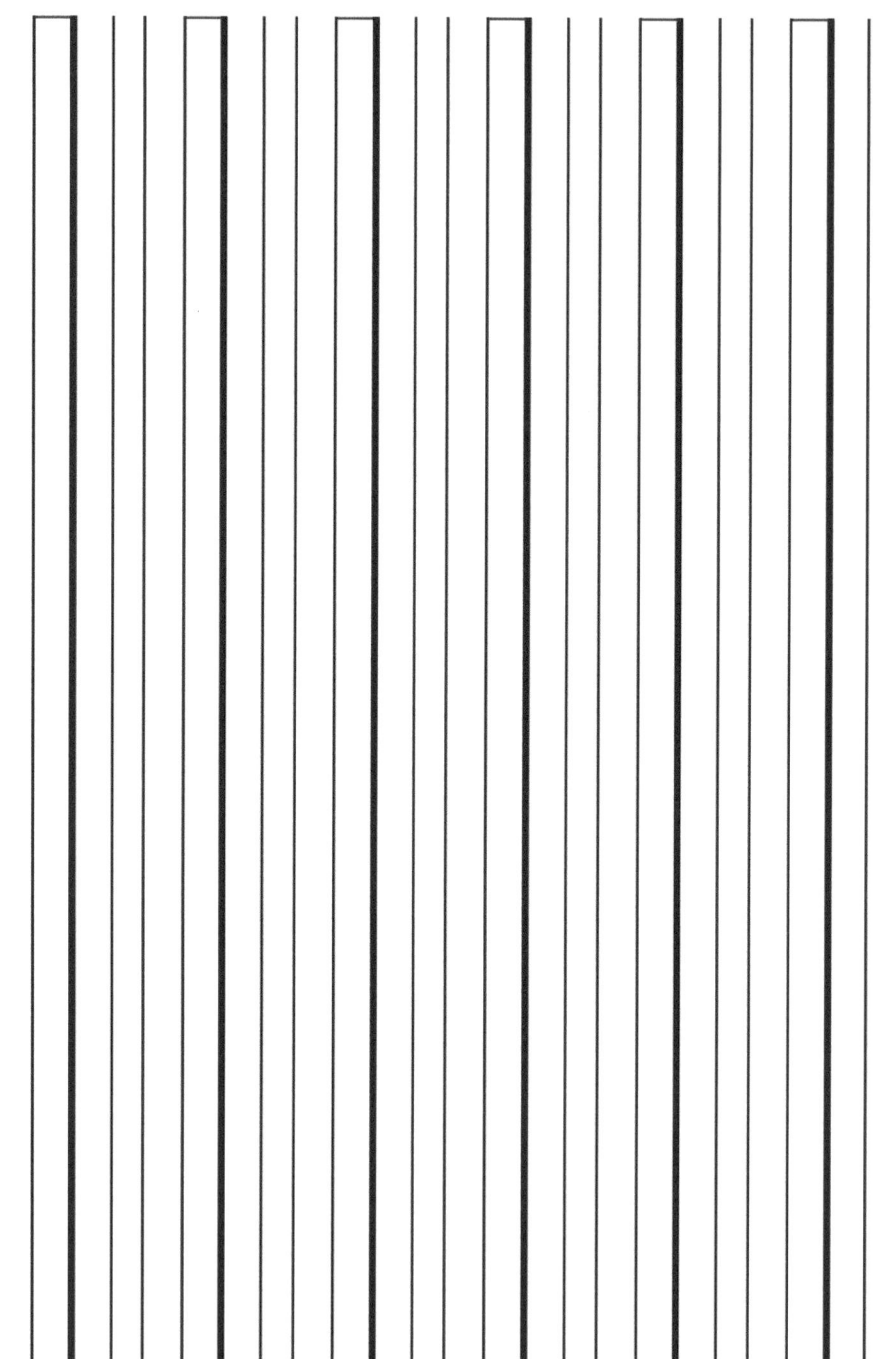

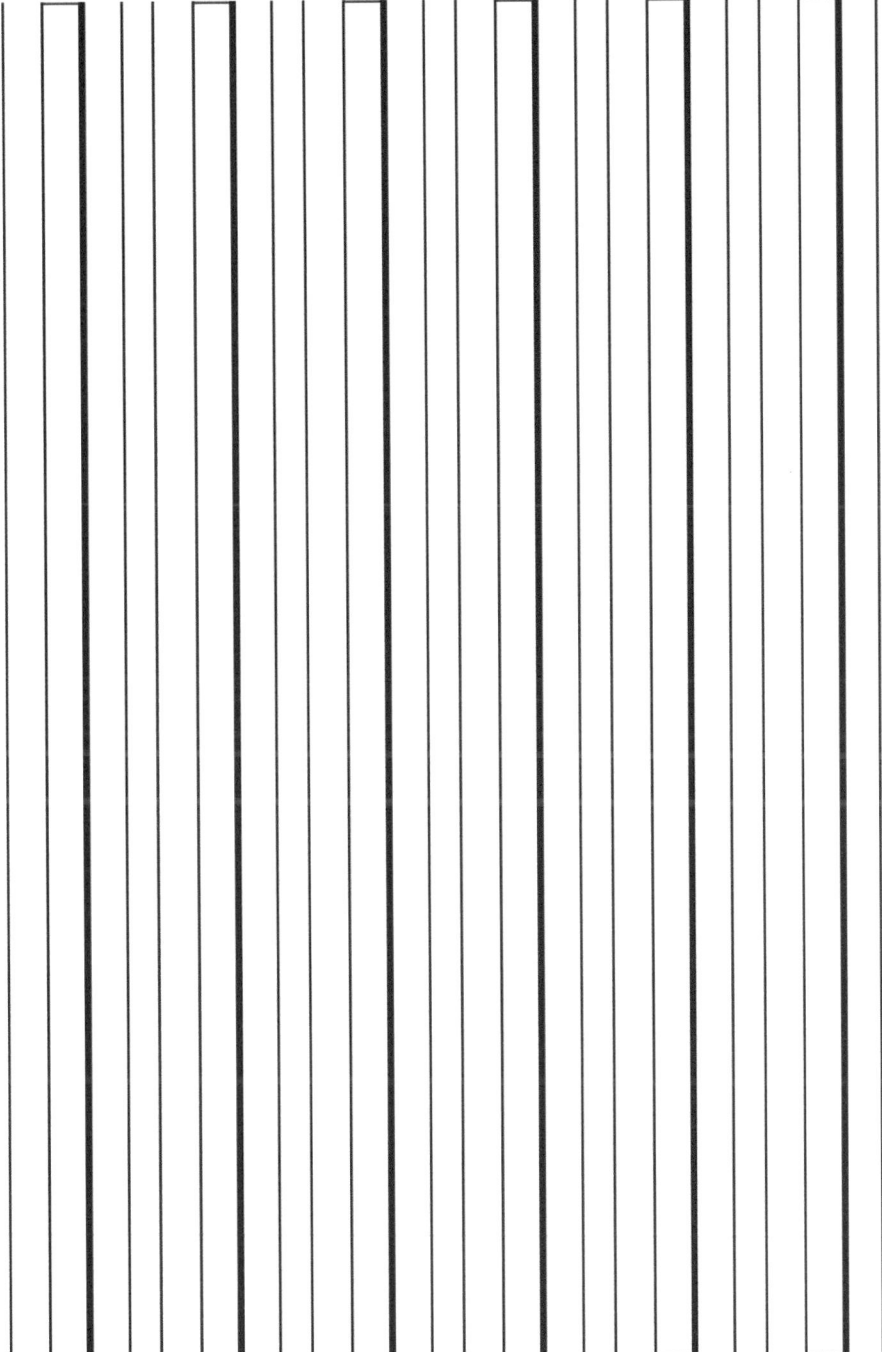

Thanks to Dr. Vera Köpsel

Susanne Dorendorff

studied graphic design, typography, font development, illustration design, calligraphy and painting. Today, she is a visual artist with a main focus on handwriting and the art of writing. Using her professional know-how to advocate a new, intellectual perception of handwriting culture, she is giving crucial impulses for moving handwriting into the consciousness of children and adults in a fear-free way. Dorendorff, whose own expressive handwriting is often used by publishers and advertisers, has developed innovative curricula and methods to train teachers in the skill of teaching children how to write. Based on her practical experiences, Susanne Dorendorff has authored several non-fiction books, developed the first method of writing teaching for boys, and is the creator of the handwriting aesthetic ASIEA. Furthermore, she is a leading expert for handwriting didactics, handwriting science and art.

Together with Susanne Dorendorff, you can learn more about handwriting and develop your own, personal perception of and find new joy in using your individual writing style.

Notes

Notes

Notes